THE KIDS' CARTOON BIBLE

ii

Other Books by Chaya M. Burstein

The Jewish Kids' Catalog
The Kids' Catalog of Israel
The Kids' Catalog of Bible Treasures

The Jewish Publication Society
Philadelphia
2002/5762

THE KIDS'
CARTOON
BIBLE

CHAYA M. BURSTEIN

The Jewish Publication Society
2100 Arch Street, 2nd floor
Philadelphia, PA 19103

Composition by Cucinotta & Associates
Design by Chaya M. Burstein
Printed in China

02 03 04 05 06 07 08 09 10   10 9 8 7 6 5 4 3 2 1

Library of Congress Cataloging-in-Publication Data

Burstein, Chaya M.
The Kids' Cartoon Bible / Chaya M. Burstein
p. cm.
Includes index.
Summary: Presents familiar stories from the Old Testament in comic strip format.
ISBN 0-8276-0729-6
1. Bible- -comic books, strips, etc. [1. Bible stories- -.T.- -Cartoons and comics.
2. Cartoons and comics.] I. Title

BS551.3 B87 2002
221.9'505- -dc21

CONTENTS

THE FIVE BOOKS OF MOSES

GENESIS

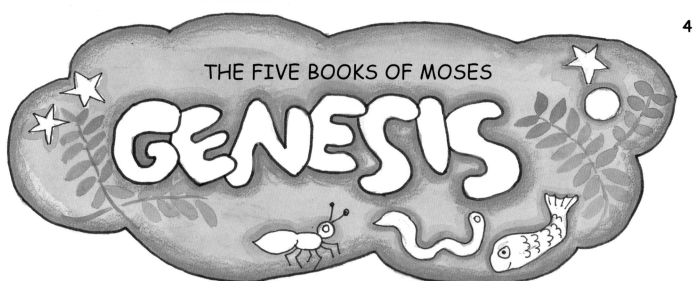

In the beginning God created heaven and earth. The earth was unformed and empty. Darkness covered the deep and a wind swept over the water. God said:

LET THERE BE LIGHT

And there was light!
God divided the light from the darkness.
God called the light Day and the darkness Night.
There was evening and there was morning.
A first day.

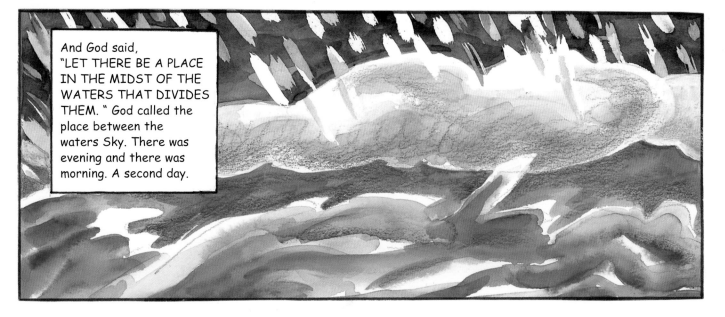

And God said, "LET THERE BE A PLACE IN THE MIDST OF THE WATERS THAT DIVIDES THEM. " God called the place between the waters Sky. There was evening and there was morning. A second day.

God said, "LET THE LOWER WATERS BE GATHERED AND LET THE DRY LAND APPEAR." God called the dry land Earth and the waters Sea.

LET GRASS AND PLANTS AND TREES GROW.

And God saw that it was good. There was evening and morning. A third day.

God said, "LET THERE BE LIGHTS IN THE SKY TO DIVIDE THE DAY FROM THE NIGHT AND TO MAKE THE SEASONS AND DAYS AND YEARS." God made a great light to rule the day and a lesser light to rule the night. There was evening and morning. A fourth day.

God blessed them, saying, "BE FRUITFUL AND MULTIPLY." And there was evening and morning. A fifth day.

God said, "LET THE EARTH BRING FORTH EVERY KIND OF LIVING CREATURE. CATTLE, CREEPING THINGS, and WILD BEASTS.

And God said, "LET US MAKE A HUMAN BEING IN OUR OWN IMAGE." Male and female God created the human being.

Now the heaven and earth were finished. God blessed the seventh day and called it holy because on that day God rested from all the work of creation.

God said to the human, "BE FRUITFUL AND MULTIPLY AND RULE THE FISH OF THE SEA, THE BIRDS OF THE AIR, AND EVERY OTHER LIVING CREATURE. THE PLANTS AND THE TREES SHALL BE FOOD FOR YOU AND FOR OTHER LIVING THINGS." God saw that everything was very good. And there was evening and morning. The sixth day.

God planted a garden in Eden. In the garden God planted trees for food and trees for beauty. In the center there was a tree of life and a tree for knowing good and evil.

TAKE CARE OF THE GARDEN. YOU MAY EAT OF EVERY TREE - BUT NOT OF THE TREE OF KNOWING GOOD AND EVIL. IF YOU EAT FROM IT YOU WILL DIE!

Yessir.. or Ma'm. Er, nossir.. or Ma'm.

God brought all the living creatures to the human being and the human gave a name to each one.

Every creature had a mate.
Only the human, Adam, had no mate.

God made Adam fall asleep.
From Adam's side God took a rib and made a woman

There was a snake in the Garden of Eden.
The snake spoke to the woman.

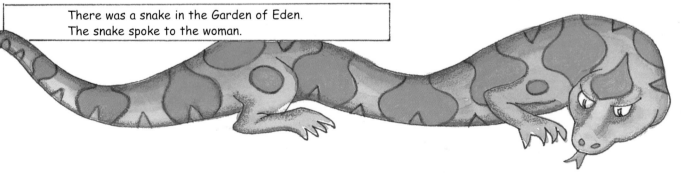

Why don't you eat from all the trees of the garden?

We can eat from some, but we're not allowed to eat from the big tree in the middle. Uh, uh. No, no!

Why not? The fruit of that tree will make you very smart.

Well... okay, just a small bite.

As they ate the fruit their eyes were suddenly opened.

Yikes! Look at us. We're naked!

Let's get some fig leaves.

Mmm... that's good. Adam, take a bite.

God knew that Adam and his mate, Eve, had sinned.

DID YOU EAT THE FORBIDDEN FRUIT?

He told me to.

She told me to.

Ha, ha - it was all my idea!

God said to the snake, "FROM NOW ON YOU ARE CURSED AND MUST CRAWL ON YOUR BELLY." To Eve God said, "YOU WILL GIVE BIRTH TO CHILDREN IN PAIN." To Adam God said, "ALL YOUR LIFE YOU WILL HAVE TO WORK HARD TO BRING FORTH FOOD FROM THE EARTH."

Then God drove Adam and Eve out of the Garden of Eden. A fiery angel guarded the gate.

Adam and Eve had two children, Cain and Abel. Cain was a farmer and Abel a hunter. They both brought gifts to God. But God accepted only Abel's gift.

One day the brothers had a fight. Cain, who was jealous, killed Abel.

God asked Cain:

WHERE IS ABEL, YOUR BROTHER?

How should I know? Am I my brother's keeper?

As punishment God sent Cain to wander across the earth. God protected him with a special mark.

The years went by and people began to behave worse and worse. They were cheats and thieves and murderers.
God said, "I'M SORRY I EVER CREATED HUMAN BEINGS! ONLY NOAH AND HIS FAMILY ARE GOOD PEOPLE."

Eve had a third son called Seth. He was the ancestor of all the other human beings until the time of Noah.

THE EARTH IS FULL OF VIOLENCE. I WILL DESTROY IT! NOAH, YOU MUST BUILD AN ARK. TAKE YOUR FAMILY AND A MALE AND FEMALE OF EVERY LIVING THING INTO THE ARK.

Noah and his family started to work.

They hammered and sawed and built a great ark.
Two by two the birds, beasts, bugs, and other living things went up into the ark.

Then the fountains of the deep burst upward and the windows of heaven opened. Rain fell for forty days and forty nights. Water covered the earth and drowned every living thing except those in the ark.

After a long time God sent a wind to blow across the waters. The rain stopped and the water began to go down.

Noah sent a raven and a dove to hunt for dry land

The dove came back with an olive branch.

COME OUT OF THE ARK! BE FRUITFUL AND MULTIPLY. I PROMISE THAT I WILL NEVER AGAIN MAKE A FLOOD TO DESTROY THE EARTH. THE RAINBOW WILL REMIND ME OF MY PROMISE.

Hallelujah!

Hurray! I was getting webbed feet already.

Many people were born after the flood. They all spoke the same language. The people settled in the land of Shinar and began to build a city.

We'll build a big, giant tower with its top in heaven!

Bigger is better.

Up! Up!

The Lord saw the tower and said, "THESE HUMANS THINK THEY CAN DO ANYTHING THEY WANT. I'LL STOP THEM BY MIXING UP THEIR WORDS."

God made each builder speak a different language. There was a babble of sounds on the tower.

Gimmee a block.

I'm getting outa here.

Vite, vite! Plus d'eau.

Vos hostu gezogt?

Veet.. ploo... what?

Paskudnyak

Idiot!

Arrivederci!

Disgusted, the people jumped down and ran off in all directions. The unfinished tower was the Tower of Babel.

God came to Abram in Ur. "GO TO THE LAND I WILL SHOW YOU," said God. "I WILL MAKE OF YOU A GREAT NATION." Abram, his wife Sarai and their nephew, Lot, journeyed to Canaan, Egypt, and back to Canaan. Lot settled in Sodom. Abram's family settled in Hebron, in Canaan.

I will build an altar to the Lord here.

Abram was sad because he had no children. God said:

COUNT THE STARS IN THE SKY. YOU WILL HAVE AS MANY CHILDREN AND CHILDREN'S CHILDREN AS THESE STARS.

Sarai wanted Abram to have a child. She gave her servant Hagar to Abram as a wife. Soon Hagar gave birth to a baby boy.

You're beautiful! I'll call you Ishmael. It means 'God has heard.'

Again God promised that Abram and Sarai would have a son. God changed their names to Abraham and Sarah.
"I AM MAKING A COVENANT WITH YOU," said God. "I AM GIVING YOU THE LAND OF CANAAN. YOU WILL BE THE FATHER OF MANY NATIONS. AS A SIGN OF THE COVENANT EVERY MALE IN YOUR FAMILY MUST BE CIRCUMCISED.

Abraham laughed:

Hey, I'm a hundred years old and my wife Sarah is ninety. How can we have a son?

Three messengers (sent by God) came to Abraham's tent. Sarah and Abraham prepared a meal for them.

When I visit you next year your wife Sarah will have a son.

A son? At my age?

Sarah laughed too.

Two of God's messengers left Abraham's tent and went to Sodom, where Lot lived. Evil people lived in Sodom and nearby Gomorrah. God decided to destroy them, but Abraham tried to save the cities.

Please God, don't destroy them. What if fifty good people live there?

IF THERE ARE FIFTY I WILL NOT DESTROY THEM.

Yeah, well... what if there are forty... or thirty... or twenty.. or ten?

But there weren't even ten good people in Sodom and Gomorrah.

When God's messengers came to Lot's house in Sodom the townspeople banged on the door.

Send out the strangers!

Kill 'em!

Let us at them.

God's messengers said to Lot, "God must destroy this evil city. You, your wife, and two daughters must get out of Sodom right now!"

Follow me. Hurry! And don't look back!

A rain of sulphur, rocks, and fire poured down on Sodom and Gomorrah. It destroyed everything. Lot and his family were saved. But Lot's wife looked back and turned into a pillar of salt.

Sarah had a baby as God had promised.

A ninety-year-old with a baby. What a joke! I'll call him Isaac, "he will laugh."

Isaac grew older and Ishmael, the son of Hagar, started teasing him. Sarah complained to Abraham.

Get rid of Hagar and Ishmael. I don't want that bully to share Isaac's birthright!

Help, Mama!

How can I send away my own son?

DO AS SARAH SAYS. ISAAC IS YOUR RIGHTFUL HEIR. DON'T WORRY, ISHMAEL WILL BE FINE. HE'LL BECOME FATHER OF A NATION.

So Abraham sent Hagar and Ishmael away.

They wandered in the desert until they ran out of water. Hagar wept, afraid that Ishmael would die. But God showed Hagar a well filled with water and promised, "DO NOT FEAR. I WILL MAKE OF ISHMAEL A GREAT NATION."

One day God decided to test Abraham.

ABRAHAM!

Here I am, having lunch.

TAKE YOUR SON ISAAC TO THE LAND OF MORIAH AND OFFER HIM TO ME AS A SACRIFICE.

gulp

The next morning Abraham, Isaac, and two servants started out for Moriah.

When they reached Moriah, Abraham and Isaac climbed the hill of sacrifice.

Papa, I see the wood and the flint, but where is the lamb for the sacrifice?

God will provide the lamb, my son.

STOP! DON'T TOUCH THE BOY!

God said, "NOW I KNOW YOU FEAR GOD AND WOULD EVEN GIVE ME YOUR FAVORITE SON. I WILL BLESS YOU AND YOU WILL HAVE AS MANY DESCENDANTS AS THE STARS IN THE HEAVENS."

Uh-oh! Now it's my turn.

Sarah died when she was 127 years old. Abraham bought a field and a cave named Mahpelah where he buried Sarah. Then he sent his servant to Aram Naharayim to find a wife for Isaac. The servant returned with Rebecca.

Rebecca gave birth to twin boys.

Esau, the first-born, was a hunter. He was Isaac's favorite.

Jacob, Rebecca's favorite, liked staying at home. He was also a good cook.

One day Esau came home and found Jacob cooking lentil soup.

I'm starving!

That soup smells terrific. Gimme some.

Let's trade. I'll give you soup and you'll give me your birth-right, so that I will inherit our father's property and position.

You got it! If I starved to death I wouldn't need the birthright anyhow.

When Isaac grew old and blind he called his son Esau.

My son, I will die soon. Before I do I want to bless you. Go out and hunt some game and make a spicy stew for me. Then I'll bless you.

Thanks Pop.

Rebecca overheard them.

This is bad news. I've got to find a way to make Isaac bless Jacob instead of Esau.

Jake, stop everything! It's an emergency. Your father wants to give Esau the birthright.

But don't worry. I have a plan.

I'll make a spicey stew. You'll bring it to your father. And you'll get the blessing instead of Esau.

Absolutely not! I can't fool Father. I don't smell like Esau. I'm not hairy like he is. I don't sound like him.

Trust me, Jake. You'll be fine. Just take off that silly hat.

Rebecca put strips of sheepskin on Jacob's arms and gave him Esau's smelly shirt to wear. Then she cooked a spicy stew and sent Jacob into the tent of Isaac, his father.

I-I am Esau, your first-born. And here is your stew. Now p-please bless me.

Strange. The voice is Jacob's, but the hands are Esau's.

Isaac ate the stew. He kissed his son and blessed him.

May God give you dew and good crops. The nations will bow down to you. Cursed be everyone who curses you. Blessed be everyone who blesses you.

Just as Jacob left Esau came rushing in

Here's your stew, Pop. Now bless me.

Esau? But...but.. I must have given your blessing to your brother.

Oh please, please find a blessing for me too.

Isaac blessed Esau saying, "You will live in rich, fruitful lands. But you will live by the sword and serve your brother until, one day, you will break loose from your brother's rule."

Esau came out of his father's tent boiling mad!

I'll kill Jacob for stealing my blessing! As soon as our father dies - I'll slaughter him!

Jake, you're in danger! Esau wants to kill you. Get out of here. Go to your uncle Laban's house.

Jacob grabbed his backpack and started out for Paddan-Aram. When he stopped to rest he dreamed he saw a ladder that stretched from the earth to heaven. Angels climbed up and down on it. God spoke to Jacob:

I AM THE LORD. I GIVE THIS LAND TO YOU AND YOUR DESCENDANTS. THEY WILL BE AS MANY AS THE DUST OF THE EARTH. I WILL BRING YOU BACK TO THIS LAND.

The Lord shall be my God.

In Paddan-Aram Jacob came to his Uncle Laban. Laban had two daughters, Leah and Rachel. Jacob fell in love with Rachel, the younger daughter.

Jacob, come and work for me. What shall I pay you?

I'll work for you for seven years for the hand of your daughter Rachel.

For seven years, in rain, storm, and burning heat Jacob tended Laban's flocks.

But on his wedding day Laban tricked Jacob and gave him Leah, the older daughter, as a wife.

Nossirree! I made a deal for Rachel.

Impossible! In Paddan-Aram a younger sister can't marry before her older sister.

Poor Jacob had to work seven more years for Rachel.

You were worth waiting for.

Leah and Rachel and their handmaidens, Zilpah and Bilhah, had lots of children.

Reuven   Gad   Asher   Dan   Simeon

Naphtali   Joseph   Dina   Levi   Judah

Benjamin   Issachar   Zebulon

Finally after twenty years it was time for Jacob and his big family, his servants and flocks to go home.

But Jacob was worried. He remembered Esau's threat.

So now I'm rich, with flocks of sheep and goats and a huge family ... but I'm scared. What if Esau still wants to kill me?

Please, God, You told me to come back to Canaan, so please protect me from Esau, my brother.

Jacob sent servants with gifts to meet Esau.

During the night an angel came and wrestled with Jacob. Finally the angel blessed Jacob and changed his name to Israel because he had struggled with God and men—and had won.

In the morning Esau and 400 men came to meet Jacob. Anxiously Jacob went ahead of his family to protect them. But Esau hugged and kissed Jacob and they both cried with joy. At last there was peace between them.

Esau went back to his home. Jacob and his family journeyed on toward Bethlehem. On the way Rachel gave birth to a second son, Benjamin, and died.

Joseph, Rachel's first child, was Jacob's favorite. Jacob made a coat of many colors for him. But Joseph's brothers hated him because he was the favorite and also because he had grand dreams.

Hey guys, listen to this. I dreamed we were tying up bundles of wheat and all of your bundles bowed down to mine.

This kid has got to go!

That's gross!

Papa's pet.

Brat!

And I had another dream. The sun and moon and eleven stars bowed to me!

Get rid of him!

Disgusting!

One day Jacob sent Joseph out to the pasture where his brothers were tending the sheep.

Here comes the show-off.

Hi, all.

Kill him!

No. Just throw him into a pit.

They jumped on Joseph, stripped off his fancy coat, and dumped him into a pit. Soon a caravan of foreign merchants passed by.

Let's sell Joseph to the merchants.

Brilliant idea!

I'll tell Papa!

help! lemme out!

Good riddance!

Bye Joey!

You won't get away with this!

The brothers dipped Joseph's coat in the blood of a goat and brought it to Jacob.

Aiyee! This is Joseph's coat. A wild animal must have killed him!

But Joseph was not dead. He had been carried to Egypt and sold to Potiphar, an officer in the Pharaoh's army. God helped Joseph, and he became overseer of Potiphar's house. But he had a big problem–

Potiphar's wife liked him too much.

Just a little kiss. Please cutie pie. My husband will never know.

No, I won't kiss you. Potiphar trusts me. It would be wrong.

No, no, a thousand times no!

No one turns me down. Kiss me, or you'll be sorry!

Potiphar's wife was so insulted when Joseph rejected her that she decided to get him into trouble.

That Hebrew slave tried to kiss me.

What?! You animal! Traitor! I'll have you thrown in jail!

But... but...

Even in prison God helped Joseph. He became the warden's helper and he explained the prisoner's dreams.

I had this weird dream.

One prisoner had been Pharaoh's cup-bearer.

I saw a grapevine with three branches.

It blossomed and grew grapes.

I squeezed the grapes and gave the juice to Pharaoh.

A wonderful dream! It means that in three days you'll be freed and go back to serving Pharaoh.

Pharaoh's baker was a prisoner too. He also had a weird dream.

Now listen to my dream.

I dreamed that I had three baskets of bread on my head and birds came and ate the bread from my baskets.

I'm sorry. Your dream means that in three days Pharaoh will hang you from a tree and birds will eat your flesh.

Joseph's predictions came true.

The cup-bearer was free.

The baker was killed.

But Joseph stayed in prison until, one night, Pharaoh had a strange dream. None of his wise men could explain it. Then the cup-bearer remembered Joseph.

Pharaoh sent for Joseph and told him the dream.

I saw seven fat cows come out of the river. Seven skinny cows came after them. And the skinny cows ate the fat cows.

Then seven fat ears of corn grew on one stalk. Seven thin ears sprouted behind them. And the thin ears swallowed the fat ears.

Your dream is a warning. God is telling you that Egypt will have seven years of good crops and then seven hungry years. You need help!

Appoint a manager who will store food during the good years, and give it out during the hungry years.

Joseph, you will be my manager.

The seven good years passed quickly. When the hungry years began, only Egypt had bread. People came from other lands to buy food.

Jacob, Joseph's father, sent his sons from Canaan to buy food. Benjamin, the youngest, didn't go because Jacob was afraid he'd lose him.

My sons, buy food so that we may live and not die.

In Egypt, Joseph recognized his brothers but they didn't recognize him.

My dear brothers.. I'm going to make you sweat!

I'll give you food this time. But if you come back for more you must bring your youngest brother.

The brothers went home with the food, but soon the sacks were empty.
Jacob said, "My sons, you must go back to Egypt to get more food."
"We can't unless we bring Benjamin. The manager said we must bring our youngest brother."

No! If I let him go I'm afraid I'll lose him — like I lost Joseph.

Don't worry, Papa. We'll take care of him.

He'll be okay.

We promise.

Back to Egypt went the brothers, along with Benjamin. Joseph prepared a feast for them.

While they ate Joseph had his servant hide a silver cup in Benjamin's sack.

At dawn the brothers left for home. Joseph sent his servant to stop them and search their sacks.

Thief! You stole my master's cup!

No, I didn't. Honest!

The rest of you may leave but the thief must stay here.

You can't keep Benjamin.

No, no! Not Benjamin. If we leave the boy here, our old father will die of sorrow.

Is my father still alive?

Joseph couldn't keep his secret any longer.

I am Joseph, your brother. Don't be afraid because you sold me to the merchant.

God planned that I should come to Egypt. God sent me here so that I could one day save our family. And God made me ruler of all of Egypt.

Come and live here. Bring our father and your families and flocks. Pharaoh will welcome you.

So Jacob and his sons, their families, and flocks came to live in the land of Goshen in Egypt.

When Jacob grew very old he called Joseph to him and said, "I will die soon, but God will be with you and bring you back to the land of your fathers." Then he called each of his sons and told them of the good times and the bad that the future would bring them.

Jacob died. His sons carried his body back to Hebron and buried it in the cave of Mahpelah with the bones of Abraham, Sarah, Isaac, Rebecca, and Leah.

Afterward they went back to live in the land of Goshen. When Joseph grew old he asked his family to bring his bones back to Canaan one day.

THE FIVE BOOKS OF MOSES

EXODUS

As the years passed, the children of Israel were fruitful and multiplied. The land was filled with them. The new Pharaoh of Egypt got worried.

There are too many Israelites! I have to stop them from multiplying.

Pharaoh set bosses over the Israelites to make them work hard. They built cities and labored in the fields, but still more and more Israelite babies were born.

Pharaoh thought and thought and suddenly had an idea.

We'll drown all the baby boys!

I'm a genius

A woman of the tribe of Levi gave birth to a boy. She hid him for three months. Then she put him in a reed basket beside the river.

His sister Miriam watched him.

In the morning, Pharaoh's daughter came to the river to bathe.

It's a baby— maybe an Israelite baby. And it's hungry. Poor thing.

Miriam jumped up.

Shall I get an Israelite nurse to feed the baby?

What a good idea!

The baby's mother nursed him and then brought him to Pharaoh's daughter in the palace.

You will be my son, and your name will be Moses, because it means "I pulled you out of the water."

Moses grew up in the palace. Once, when he went for a walk...

...he saw an Egyptian beating an Israelite slave. Moses jumped on the Egyptian and killed him.

Then Moses ran away to the land of Midian. There he married Zipporah and quietly tended his father-in-law Jethro's flocks.

Back in Egypt the Jews were suffering. They cried to God for help, and God decided to send for Moses.

One day Moses found a bush burning in the pasture.

What's happening? The bush burns and burns – but it doesn't burn up!

God spoke to Moses out of the bush.

I AM THE GOD OF YOUR FATHERS. MY NAME IS 'I-AM-WHO-I-WAS-AND-WILL-BE.' I WILL DELIVER MY PEOPLE FROM THE EGYPTIANS AND BRING THEM TO A LAND OF MILK AND HONEY. TELL PHARAOH TO LET THE ISRAELITES GO!

After that Pharaoh gave the Israelites more work than ever.

They yelled at Moses and Aaron because their work was harder.

Moses complained to God. "Why did you send me to Pharaoh? Now the people are worse off than before."

TRUST ME. I MADE A COVENANT WITH ABRAHAM, ISAAC AND JACOB TO BRING YOU TO THE LAND OF CANAAN. I WILL FREE YOU FROM SLAVERY IN EGYPT.

Yeah, yeah!

We heard *that* before

*We want action!

All the time—promises!

God said, "GO BACK TO PHARAOH AND SHOW HIM YOUR POWER."

Look here Pharaoh, God gave me this magic stick.

"That's nothing!" cried Pharaoh's magicians. They threw down their own sticks, which turned into snakes. But the snake-stick of Moses ate up all the others.

That's just a silly trick. I won't let the Israelites go. **Forget it!**

MOSES, TELL PHARAOH AGAIN TO LET MY PEOPLE GO. IF HE REFUSES, STRIKE THE STICK AGAINST THE WATER OF THE RIVER.

"No!" said Pharaoh.
Aaron struck the water. It turned red as blood and stank. All the fish died. For seven days no one could drink it.

Again Moses went to Pharaoh and said, "Let my people go!" Again Pharaoh said, "Never!" So God sent a plague of frogs to infest Egypt.

Okay, okay! I'll let them go. Just get these frogs off me!

As soon as the frogs were gone Pharaoh changed his mind and said, "No way! The Israelites stay!"
God sent swarms of gnats and flies.
Only the land of Goshen, where the Israelites lived, was free of them.

God caused a plague that killed the cattle. Then boils broke out on the Egyptians. Then hail, rain, and thunder crushed the land. Next, locusts blew in and ate every green leaf.

After each plague Pharaoh promised to let the Israelites go but quickly changed his mind.

The ninth plague brought three days of darkness to all the land of Egypt, except where the Israelites lived.

When Pharaoh still refused, God sent the most terrible plague of all—the death of the first-born.

Israelites, smear lamb's blood on your doorposts. In the same night you must roast and eat the entire lamb.

That night the Lord passed over the houses that had blood on their doorposts. In all the other houses the first-born died.

Finally Pharaoh gave up.

Get out! Take your children and your flocks and go — before we're all dead!

"Remember this day," Moses told his people. "Each year at this season you shall eat matzah, un-leavened bread, for seven days, to remember that God brought you out of the land of Egypt."

The people hurried into the wilderness. They carried the bones of Joseph to bury in Canaan.

A pillar of cloud led them by day.	A pillar of fire lit their way by night.

But God hardened Pharaoh's heart.

I want those slaves back!

Men, let's go get 'em!

We'll trap them at the shore of the sea.

Oh God! Here come the Egyptians.

Help!

I give up! Better to be a live slave than a drowned hero.

They'll kill us!

I can't swim!

Moses stretched out his stick over the Sea of Reeds.

Go forward into the water. God will fight for you.

The waters divided and the Israelites crossed over on dry land between the two walls of water.

When Pharaoh and his army followed, the water poured back and drowned them all.

Moses' sister Miriam led happy singing and dancing to celebrate God's victory.

Then the long walk through the desert began. When the Israelites were thirsty, God showed Moses how to turn salt water into sweet water. When they were hungry, the Lord provided manna for breakfast and quail for dinner. But how they complained!

I'm tired. Are we there yet?

Ouch! My blister hurts.

I'm hungry. When do we eat?

Forget it! We'll only get manna again.

I knew I shoulda stayed in Goshen.

When the Israelites camped at Rephidim, a people called Amalekites attacked them. Moses sent fighters led by Joshua to face the enemy.

Moses watched from a hilltop. When his arms were up, the Israelites began to win. When he got tired and dropped them, the Amalekites won. Finally Aaron and Hur held up Moses' weary arms until the sun set, and Israel won.

Jethro, the father of Moses' wife, Zipporah, brought Zipporah and her two sons to join Moses.

Papa!

My son, don't judge everyone all by yourself. Appoint judges to help you.

Jethro gave Moses good advice on how to run the camp.

You're right. I'll do it.

Jethro went home and the Israelites marched on into the grim wilderness of Sinai.

They camped before a great, gray mountain called Mount Sinai.
From out of the clouds at the top of the mountain,
God said to Moses:

TELL THE PEOPLE TO KEEP MY COVENANT, AND THEY WILL BE A HOLY NATION.

We will! We will! We'll do whatever you say!

Now you must bathe and purify yourselves. In three days God will speak to you again.

On the third day smoke and clouds covered the mountain. Lightening blazed. Shrill blasts of the shofar, the ram's horn, made the mountain tremble. The people trembled too.

Out of the thunder God spoke to Moses and gave him Ten Commandments. Moses repeated the commandments to the Israelites.

I AM THE LORD, YOUR GOD. YOU SHALL NOT WORSHIP ANY OTHER GOD.

YOU SHALL NOT MAKE STATUES OR PICTURES OF LIVING THINGS IN ORDER TO PRAY TO THEM.

DO NOT USE MY NAME TO SWEAR FALSELY.

REMEMBER THE SABBATH DAY TO KEEP IT HOLY FOR YOU, YOUR FAMILY, SERVANTS, GUESTS AND WORK ANIMALS.

HONOR YOUR FATHER AND YOUR MOTHER.

DO NOT KILL ANYONE.

DO NOT TAKE ANOTHER MAN'S WIFE OR ANOTHER WOMAN'S HUSBAND.

DO NOT STEAL.

DO NOT LIE ABOUT YOUR NEIGHBOR.

DO NOT WANT A THING THAT BELONGS TO YOUR NEIGHBOR.

God also gave Moses a list of laws to guide the people so that they would treat each other justly and kindly.

MOSES, COME UP TO THE MOUNTAINTOP. I WILL GIVE YOU THE TABLETS OF THE TEN COMMANDMENTS AND THE LAWS.

Aaron, I gotta go up. Take care of things while I'm gone.

Sure. No problem.

Aaron melted down the gold and shaped it into a calf. The Israelites danced happily around the golden calf and worshipped it.

Meanwhile, up on the mountain God was giving Moses more laws and also instructions for conducting services and for building an Ark, a cabinet to hold the tablets of the Ten Commandments.

God gave Moses the two stone tablets carved with the Ten Commandments and then, after forty days and nights of hard listening, Moses started down the mountain. Suddenly he stopped.

What's that? A golden calf? My people are praying to a statue!

In a fury Moses threw down the tablets and smashed them!

These people have sinned greatly, God. Will You forgive them?

THEY ARE A STIFF-NECKED PEOPLE AND THEY WILL SUFFER. BUT YOU WILL LEAD THEM TO THE PROMISED LAND. CARVE TWO NEW TABLETS AND BRING THEM UP TO THE MOUNTAIN.

After another forty days and nights Moses brought down the inscribed tablets and God's message. His face shone so brightly that Aaron and the people were frightened.

Moses had to wear a veil to calm them down.

Then they began to build God's Tabernacle which would hold the Ark and the Commandments.

They spun and wove the finest linen, goat, and camel's hair. They dyed the fabrics brilliant purples, and crimsons, and blues for wall hangings.

Then they wove a tent to house the Tabernacle and the Ark. This was the Tent of Meeting.

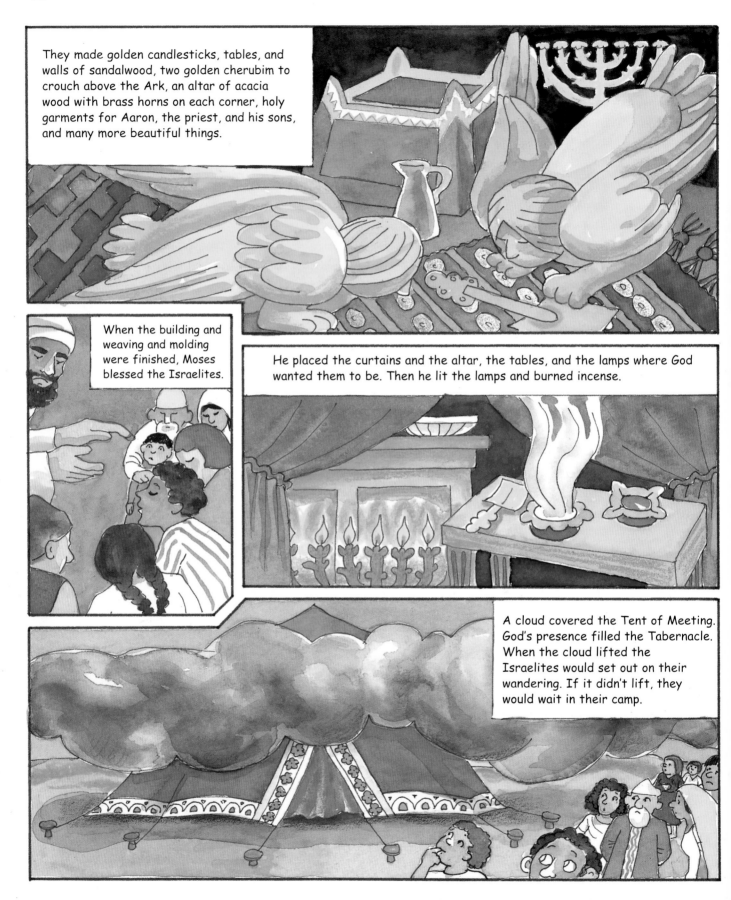

They made golden candlesticks, tables, and walls of sandalwood, two golden cherubim to crouch above the Ark, an altar of acacia wood with brass horns on each corner, holy garments for Aaron, the priest, and his sons, and many more beautiful things.

When the building and weaving and molding were finished, Moses blessed the Israelites.

He placed the curtains and the altar, the tables, and the lamps where God wanted them to be. Then he lit the lamps and burned incense.

A cloud covered the Tent of Meeting. God's presence filled the Tabernacle. When the cloud lifted the Israelites would set out on their wandering. If it didn't lift, they would wait in their camp.

THE FIVE BOOKS OF MOSES

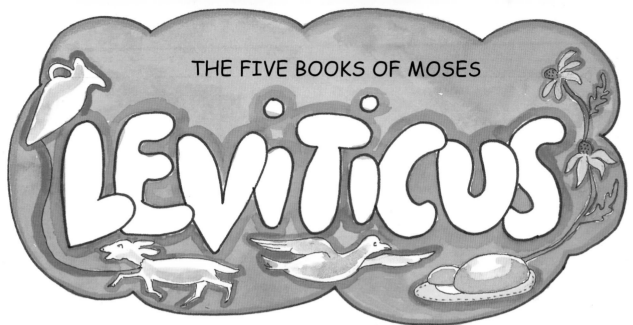

LEVITICUS

God called Moses to the Tent of Meeting, saying:

OFFERINGS TO THE LORD SHALL BE OF CATTLE, SHEEP, GOATS, DOVES OR FLOUR. THE FIRE ON MY ALTAR MUST BURN DAY AND NIGHT. PART OF THESE OFFERINGS WILL BE FOR THE PRIESTS.

For seven days Aaron and his sons sat in the Tent of Meeting. On the eighth day they placed their offering on the altar. Fire came from the Lord and burned it.

Moses dressed Aaron and his sons in their priestly garments and anointed them with oil.

God told Moses and Aaron which foods were permitted and which were forbidden. "YOU MAY NOT EAT UNCLEAN FOODS BECAUSE YOU MUST BE HOLY, JUST AS I AM HOLY," said God.

God gave the Israelites laws about curing illnesses, about childbirth, about observing Shabbat and holidays, and more. "LOVE YOUR NEIGHBOR AND THE STRANGER AMONG YOU AS YOU LOVE YOURSELF," said God. "LEAVE THE HARVEST IN THE CORNERS OF THE FIELD FOR THE POOR. BE HONEST IN BUSINESS. JUDGE EVERYONE FAIRLY."

THE FIVE BOOKS OF MOSES
NUMBERS

Moses counted the people in the tribes of Israel. Then each tribe walked under its own banner and camped in its own place near the Tent of Meeting.

The Israelites ate roasted quail, boiled quail, quail burgers, quail quiche, quail salad, quail pudding...

Ugh... quail again? It's coming out of my ears!

At last the tribes reached the southern border of Canaan, the Promised Land.

Hallelujah! Hurray We made it! / we're terrific!

Calm down! We still have work to do. A man from each tribe must go into Canaan to spy out the land.

Moses said, "Find out if the land is fruitful, if the people are strong, if there are walled cities. And bring back some fruit of the land."

For forty days the spies explored the Land of Canaan. From south to north. From east to west.

They came back staggering under a load of gigantic fruit.

Only two of the spies, Joshua and Caleb, were not afraid. The Israelites panicked. Some of them began to throw stones.

God spoke angrily from the Tent of Meeting.

HOW LONG WILL YOU DISOBEY ME? AND HAVE NO FAITH IN ME? I WILL DISOWN YOU. I WILL STRIKE YOU WITH A PLAGUE!

No, God. Please forgive this people.

I'LL FORGIVE THEM BUT NONE OF THEM SHALL LIVE TO SEE THE PROMISED LAND! ONLY THEIR CHILDREN WILL GO IN. NOW TURN AND MARCH BACK INTO THE WILDERNESS.

As the tribes wandered on through the desert, Korah of the tribe of Levi, rebelled against Moses.

What makes you so special, Moses? We're all holy. Who are you that you're always giving us orders?

Uh oh! Korach's in BIG trouble.

Moses, Aaron, Korah, and his supporters stood before the Tent.

At that moment the earth under Korah and his followers burst open!

They and all their possessions were swallowed up. The earth closed over them and they vanished.

After that there was no more muttering against God.

Sometimes the Israelites reached the lands of other people who refused to let them pass through. They had to fight the king of Arad, the Canaanites, the Amorites, and others in order to pass.

When the Israelites reached the border of Moab, the King of Moab became frightened. He sent a message to a famous magician named Balaam.

Come to Moab to curse the Israelites and make them weak. I'll pay you lots of gold if you succeed.

Balaam started out. On the way Balaam's donkey suddenly saw an angel standing in the road. The angel was invisible to Balaam.

The donkey ran off the road.

Hey! What are you doing?

Ouch!

The donkey squeezed Balaam's leg against a wall.

Finally the donkey lay down on the road.

Get up, you idiot! What's wrong with you?

Then God let the donkey speak.

Why are you hitting me? Haven't I always been your good servant?

Yes, but now you're acting crazy. I'll beat you till . . . oops!

An angel! You're the reason my donkey would not move.

God sent me to warn you. You may go to meet the King of Moab. But you must say only what God tells you.

The king took Balaam to the top of a mountain. He looked down on the Israelites

See, that's them. Now curse them!

Three times Balaam tried to curse the Israelites. But each time God put blessings into his mouth instead.

How fair are your tents, O Jacob! Your dwellings, O Israel! Blessed are they who bless you. Cursed are they who curse you.

The king of Moab was disgusted.

I wanted curses, not blessings! You won't get a penny from me. Go home!

The tribes of Israel camped on the mountain slopes of Moab, facing Jericho. God told Moses where the borders of Canaan would be. The Israelites were commanded to drive out the people who lived in Canaan. Then the land would be divided among the tribes of Israel. And Joshua would lead them after Moses died.

THE FIVE BOOKS OF MOSES

DEUTERONOMY

In the fortieth year of wandering, the Israelites reached the east side of the Jordan River, opposite the Land of Canaan. Moses retold the story of their wandering in the desert.

Remember when God spoke to you out of the fire and gave you rules and commandments.

Remember when you were afraid to enter Canaan and went back to the desert? That frightened generation has died and now the generation born in the desert will go into the land.

Again Moses taught his people the law.

Keep the Sabbath and My holy days. Appoint judges to govern and guarantee justice. Protect the rights of strangers, the fatherless and widows. Set up cities of refuge for those who have killed a person accidentally. Eat only kosher food . . . . . . and many more laws.

Moses repeated the Ten Commandments. "Amen," said the people.

When you come into the land of Canaan, destroy the pagan altars and high places. Build a central altar where you will worship God and bring offerings. Rejoice and feast there before God.

God is bringing you into a good land, with streams and springs.
A land of wheat and barley, of vines, figs, and pomegranates.
A land of olive trees and honey.

Blessed shall be your children, your fields, and your flocks. You will succeed if you faithfully observe God's commandments.

If you do not obey God, you will be cursed.

Then Moses told the people:

I am 120 years old. I can't lead you any more. But God will march with you across the Jordan. And Joshua will lead you.

In the Tent of Meeting God appeared in a cloud and spoke to Joshua.

BE STRONG AND COURAGEOUS! YOU WILL BRING THE ISRAELITES INTO THEIR LAND. AND I WILL BE WITH YOU.

Moses left Joshua and climbed high up to the top of Mount Nebo.

From there God showed him the Land of Canaan. Then Moses died and God buried him in a secret place.

For thirty days the people mourned him. A prophet like Moses never again appeared in Israel. Moses, who spoke to God face to face.

THE BOOK OF PROPHETS

JOSHUA

God spoke to Joshua.

YOU WILL LEAD THE ISRAELITES OVER THE JORDAN RIVER TO THE LAND I HAVE GIVEN YOU. BE STRONG AND COURAGEOUS.

Yippee!

Must we?

So soon?

Hurray! Yeah!

Finally!

Israelites, prepare yourselves. In three days we will cross the Jordan and take the land!

You and you— sneak into Jericho and spy out the city.

The spies went to Jericho and lodged in the house of a woman named Rahav.

The king of Jericho sent men to Rahav to capture the Israelites. She hid the spies on the roof.

Where are the spies who came to your house?

They went that way, out of the city. Hurry! You may catch them.

I hid you because I know God is with you. So please save me and my family when your soldiers come to conquer the city.

When the Israelites attack, hang a red cord from this window. Everyone in your house will be safe.

Rahav let the spies down from the window and they escaped across the river.

The spies reported to Joshua.

The people of Jericho are scared of us

Good! Let's go!

The priests and the Ark went into the river first.

As they stepped in, the Jordan River stopped flowing. The priests and the Ark waited in the middle of the dry river bed until all the Israelites reached the opposite bank.

When the priests and the Ark reached shore, the river began to flow again.

On the plains of Jericho, the Israelites circumcised the men who had been born in the desert. Manna stopped falling, and the people ate the wheat and grain of the land. And then God told Joshua how to conquer Jericho.

Every day for six days the Israelites walked once around the city walls. First the soldiers, then seven priests blowing on shofars, then the priests carrying the Ark of the Covenant, then more soldiers and all the people.

On the seventh day they began to walk at dawn. They circled the walls seven times. On the seventh walk-around the priests blasted on their shofars and the people shouted a great shout.

The walls of Jericho fell down.

The Israelite soldiers charged into the city. They conquered it and destroyed it completely.

Only Rahav and her family were saved.

After Jericho, the Israelites battled to conquer other cities in Canaan. Many kings joined forces to fight Israel. Their soldiers were as many as the grains of sand on the seashore. But with God's help, the Israelites won city after city until, finally, they were finished and the land rested from war.

Joshua was an old man when the fighting stopped. But he still had one important job to do.

I must divide the land of Canaan among the tribes of Israel. And from its portion each tribe will give land and cities to the priestly tribe of Levi.

THE BOOK OF PROPHETS

JUDGES

Many young Israelites forgot their parents' promises to God and Joshua. They began to follow the customs of their Canaanite neighbors.

Some married their non-Israelite neighbors.

Some of them worshipped idols.

God's anger burned against them. When other nations attacked them, stole from them, and enslaved them, God would not help the Israelites. But when they became totally miserable, God took pity on them and appointed judges to lead them.

Samson, Deborah, and Gideon were judges.

Sisera, the Canaanite general, came thundering down from the north with 900 iron chariots.

There's easy pickings here!

He oppressed and plundered the Israelites.

Oh God, where are You when we need You?

Deborah, the judge, liked to sit peacefully under a palm tree and judge the people.

But as Sisera came closer and got meaner, she knew she'd have to stop him.

She called in a powerful fighter named Barak.

You must gather an army and fight Sisera!

If you come with me I'll do it.

If you need my help in battle you're not a big hero. Someone else will kill Sisera.

That's okay.

Deborah and Barak quickly led the Israelite army up the slope of Mount Tabor.

Sisera and his 900 chariots and thousands of archers, horsemen, and foot soldiers filled the valley below. The Kishon Brook ran between the two armies.

Ha! We've got them trapped like rats!

Deborah, when should we attack?

When I raise my arms.

As the armies glared at each other, a small cloud appeared in the sky. It grew and grew and turned black as charcoal.

it grew and grew and grew!

Suddenly rain started to pour down. Deborah raised her arms and Barak yelled:

Charge!

Israelite arrows stabbed into the crowded Canaanite soldiers. Rain filled the Kishon Brook. It overflowed and poured into the valley. The chariot wheels sank deep into the mud.

Sisera's horses and men slipped and slid and crashed into each other...

...and finally they gave up and ran away.

67

Sisera ran also. He found shelter in the tent of Yael the Kenite. She gave him milk to drink, let him rest and then POW! She killed him.

"Oh Lord, when You marched out, the earth trembled and the heavens dropped," Deborah sang gratefully to God. And the land was quiet for forty years.

God, help us

Again the Israelites began to pray to strange gods and to treat each other badly. And again God stopped protecting them. The Midianites invaded the land with hordes of camels and cattle and ate everything in sight.

An angel of the Lord came to Gideon of the Tribe of Manasseh.

Gideon, wake up! Go and save Israel from the Midianites!

The Lord said:

SEND SOME OF THESE MEN HOME. I'LL SAVE ISRAEL WITH ONLY 300 FIGHTERS.

HELP!

Gideon sounded the horn, and people came from all the tribes, ready to fight.

That night God told Gideon to attack the Midianite camp. Gideon went to the camp to listen secretly to the enemy. And he came back with a plan.

The Midianites were quickly defeated and made peace with Israel. But soon the Philistines marched in and oppressed the Israelites. At that time a baby was born to a woman of the tribe of Dan.
An angel of God told her:

This baby is a Nazirite. He is holy to God. You must never cut his hair and he must never drink wine. When he grows up he will free Israel from the Philistines.

You're a cute, little Nazirite. I'll call you Samson.

Samson grew into a large, powerful man.

But he had no luck with women. First he fell in love with a Philistine woman.

When she married someone else, Samson took revenge. He caught 300 foxes, tied burning torches to their tails, and set them loose in the fields of the Philistines.

The fields burned to the ground. When the Philistines came after him, Samson grabbed a donkey's jawbone and killed a thousand men.

Then Samson fell in love again, with a woman named Delilah.

Philistines said to Delilah:

We'll pay you 1100 shekels if you'll find out what makes Samson so strong.

Sammy, honey, what makes you so strong? Can anything take away your strength?

Try tying me up with strips of fresh leather.

When Samson fell asleep Delilah tied him up. Then she yelled, "Get up Samson! The Philistines are coming!"

Samson jumped up, breaking all the leather strips.

"You lied to me! If you really loved me, you'd tell me what will make you weak."

"But I *do* love you. Honestly I do!"

Delilah kept begging until Samson finally told her the real secret of his strength-the fact that his hair had never been cut.

When Samson fell asleep again, Delilah called the Philistines. They carefully cut off his hair and tied him up. Then she cried:

"Get up, Samson! The Philistines are attacking!"

Poor Samson was powerless.

The Philistines gouged out Samson's eyes and took him to their city of Gaza, where he worked as a slave.

Slowly his hair began to grow back.

One day there was a big party in the temple of the Philistine god, Dagon. They brought Samson so that they could make fun of him.

Samson stood between two pillars and prayed to God.

"Oh God, give me the strength to take revenge on the Philistines."

He pushed with all his might. The pillars crumbled, and the roof crashed down. Samson and his enemies died together.

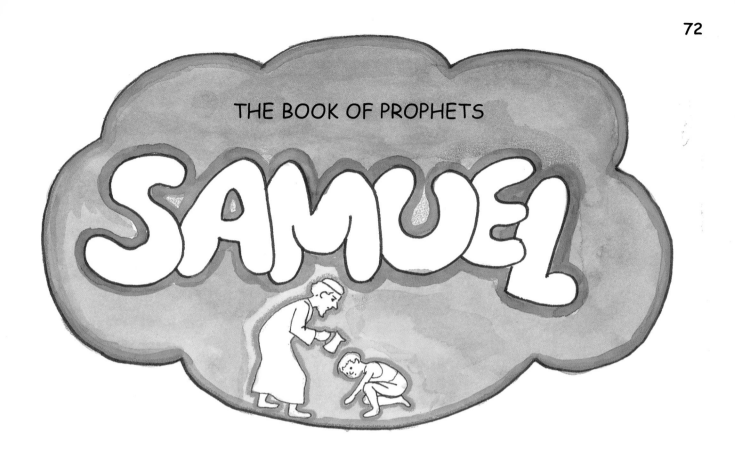

THE BOOK OF PROPHETS

SAMUEL

Hannah the wife of Elkana had no children. Year after year she came to God's sanctuary in Shiloh and prayed for a child.

Dear God, if You will give me a son I'll give him back to You to serve You all the days of his life.

At last Hannah gave birth to a baby boy.

Thank You, thank You, God. The baby's name will be Samuel because "God heard" my plea.

When Hannah finished nursing the boy, she brought him to Eli, the high priest, to serve God in Shiloh.

Eli had two sons, who were selfish and bossy.

Polish the candlesticks. Move it!

Sam, mop up the blood around the altar - Now!

The sons were bad priests. They cheated the worshippers by taking more than their fair share of the offerings.

Mmm... good bread!

Wait! There's nothing left for my family.

God decided to punish Eli's sons. One night God called Samuel.

SAMUEL!

Samuel ran to the high priest.

Did you call me, Eli?

No, my son. Go back to sleep.

SAMUEL!

Again Samuel ran to Eli.

You called? Here I am.

No, Samuel. I did not call. Go to sleep already.

God called a third time. This time Eli realized that it was God who was calling. "Go and lie down. If God calls again, say, 'Speak, Lord. Your servant is listening,'" Eli told Samuel.

"SAMUEL!" God called again.

S-s-speak, Lord. Your servant is listening.

God said, "I WILL PUNISH THE FAMILY OF THE HIGH PRIEST ELI BECAUSE HIS SONS DO EVIL AND ELI DOES NOT STOP THEM. I WILL NEVER FORGIVE THEM."

Samuel grew and God favored him. All the Israelites knew that Samuel was a prophet.

God talks to him-like person to person.

No kidding!

Once the Israelites went to fight the Philistines. They lost the battle and ran back to Shiloh.

Yeah!

If we had the ark with us we would've won. God wouldn't let us lose the ark.

Let's take it next time.

Eli's two sons went with the Ark to fight the Philistines.

The Israelites lost again. The Philistines captured the Ark, and Eli's sons were killed. The terrible news killed Eli.

Soon the Philistines were sorry they had won the Ark.

Get rid of the ark!

Wherever it stood, their gods were knocked down and their people grew ugly bumps and boils.

So the Ark came home to Shiloh.

Samuel was now the high priest in Shiloh. He said to his people:

Throw out the foreign idols. Return to God. Only God can protect you.

Amen!

The Israelites served God the whole time that Samuel was high priest.

Samuel's two sons served as priests, but they were unjust and corrupt. When Samuel grew old the people demanded a change.

Your sons are crooks! We need a king.

A king for Israel!

We want a king.

Get us a king like other nations have. A queen too!

That's a terrible idea!

A king will tax you and turn you into servants. You'll hate having a king.

A king! a king! a king!! Get us a king!!

Everyone yelled and argued until God finally said:

LET THEM HAVE A KING!

God picked a handsome, shy, young herdsman called Saul, from the tribe of Benjamin.

You will be King of Israel!!

Who? Me?

Saul surprised everyone by becoming a strong leader in battle against the Ammonites, the Philistines, and other enemies. But Saul made God angry when he disobeyed God's command.

God found a new king for Israel, a red-headed shepherd and harp player named David. Samuel anointed him secretly so that Saul didn't know.

King Saul became frightened and angry because God had left him. Saul's servant called David to play the harp and calm the king.

Saul liked the music and he liked David... at first.

The Philistines invaded Israel again. Goliath, a giant Philistine warrior, challenged the Israelite soldiers.

David came to the Israelite camp to visit his brothers. He heard Goliath's challenge.

It was a great victory. King Saul invited David to live at the palace. And Jonathan, Saul's son, became David's best friend.

David led Israel's army and won many battles. One day Saul heard the people shout words that worried him.

Saul killed thousands! But David killed tens of thousands!

Soon David will want to overthrow me and become king. I must stop him!

As David was playing for Saul the king suddenly threw his spear at him.

David ducked. Then he ran.

David and Jonathan met secretly.

Don't ever come back here, my friend. My father will kill you!

I'll never forget you. We'll always be friends.

Saul and his soldiers hunted for David all through the land. David ran from hiding place to hiding place. Meanwhile, back in Judah, the Prophet Samuel died.

Suddenly a great army of Philistines invaded Israel again. Saul's army had grown weak and he was afraid.

How can I fight them? My men are unprepared. What should I do?

I need advice and help. I need Samuel. But Samuel is dead!

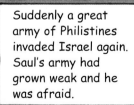
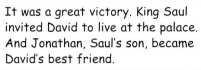

That night Saul went to the cave of a medium, a woman who could bring up the spirit of the dead.

I must speak to Samuel! Make his spirit come and talk to me.

SAMUEL

Spirit of Samuel, Saul must speak to you.

WHY DO YOU DISTURB ME?

I need you, Samuel. I'm afraid of the Philistines and God isn't helping me. What should I do?

GOD IS NOT WITH YOU. THE PHILISTINES WILL KILL YOU. DAVID WILL BE KING

Samuel's frightening words came true. Saul, Jonathan, and Saul's other sons were killed in battle against the Philistines.

David cried for them.

How are the mighty fallen. Saul and Jonathan were loved in their lives, and in their deaths were not divided. They were swifter than eagles, stronger than lions. Oh my brother Jonathan, you were so dear to me.

The leaders of Israel made an agreement with David before the Lord. They anointed him as the new king.

David brought the Ark of the Covenant up to Jerusalem. Through the Prophet Nathan, God told David that God would always protect him and his house. And David's children would build a house for the Lord in Jerusalem.

Let your name be great and glorious forever.

One evening David was cooling off on the roof of his house. He saw a woman bathing on a nearby roof.

Wow! She's gorgeous. Who is that woman?

She's Bathsheba, wife of Uriah. He's one of your soldiers on the battlefront in Ammon.

I want to meet her. Bring her to me.

Bathsheba came to David. They made love and she became pregnant.

Pregnant? That's terrible! Now what will I do?

Then David had an idea.

David called Uriah back from the battlefront, pretending that he wanted news of the war. After the report David said:

Uriah, go and visit your wife.

How can I go to my wife when my comrades are fighting on the battlefront? I'll sleep here in front of the palace.

Uriah, go home! That's an order.

But I can't, your majesty.

This man is too loyal for his own good.

Uriah, I'm sending you back to Ammon with this sealed message for my commander, Joab.

To Joab, Send Uriah into the hottest part of the battle and let him be killed.

D.

Joab followed the king's orders.

Many years later Absalom, one of David's sons, rebelled against his father's rule.

All of you tribes of Israel, come and join me. I will be a better king than my father.

As Absalom's forces grew, David and his followers escaped from Jerusalem. They gathered the army for battle near the Jordan River. David gave his generals a last order:

Don't kill my son Absolom. Protect him, for my sake.

The two armies met in the dark forest of Ephraim. They fought fiercely. David's army won and Absalom raced away.

His long hair caught on a low-hanging branch. As he hung helpless, David's general and soldiers stabbed him to death.

Oh Absolom my son, oh my son! If only I had died instead of you.

Many more battles followed. David conquered Jerusalem and made it the capital of Israel. David wanted to build a Temple for the Ark but God told him his hands were too bloody with war. His son Solomon would build the Temple.

THE BOOK OF PROPHETS

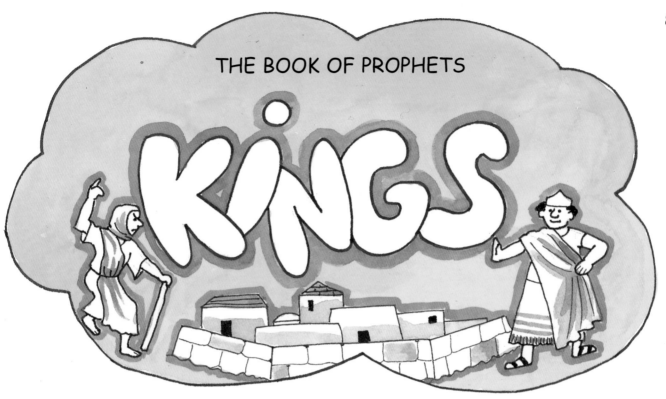

KINGS

When David grew old, he appointed Solomon, son of Bathsheba, to be the new king of Israel.

My son, I will soon go the way of all the earth. Be strong, walk in God's ways and you will prosper.

After David died Solomon went to worship God in Gibeon. He had a dream.

SOLOMON, WHAT SHALL I GIVE YOU?

God, being a king is a very hard job. I'm not sure I can do it. Please give me an understanding heart to judge Your people.

I WILL GIVE YOU AN UNDERSTANDING HEART, WISDOM AND ALSO WEALTH AND HONOR. FOLLOW MY COMMANDMENTS AS DAVID DID (most of the time) AND I WILL GRANT YOU A LONG LIFE.

Back in Jerusalem two women came to Solomon for judgment.

All of Israel heard of Solomon's wisdom. They feared and respected him. He was king of a rich land that lived at peace with its neighbors.

The Israelites lived peacefully under their grape-vines and fig trees, from Dan to Beersheba, all the days of Solomon.

My father wanted to build a temple to God, but he was at war all the time. Now that there is peace I'll build the Temple.

Solomon sent a message to Hiram, king of Tyre, a land of tall cedar and cypress trees. He wrote, "Send me cypress and cedar wood. I will send you grain as payment."

Solomon's workers cut stone in the mountains.

Hiram floated the wood over the sea to Israel on barges and rafts.

And 480 years after the children of Israel left Egypt, they laid the foundation stones for the House of the Lord in Jerusalem.

It was built according to the Lord's instructions, with an inner shrine where the Ark stood and with outer halls and courtyards.

There were altars and a great bronze basin where the priests washed their hands. There were tall columns and finely carved walls covered with gold.

When the House of the Lord was ready, the priests carried the Ark containing the stone Tablets up to the inner shrine of the Temple, the Holy of Holies.

The people gathered in the courtyard. King Solomon praised God and blessed the people.

There is no God like You, Who blesses the people and keeps promises. Hear our prayers when we turn toward this Temple, even when we are in faraway lands.

God answered, "THIS TEMPLE IS HOLY TO ME. KEEP MY LAWS AND I WILL ALWAYS BE WITH YOU."

Solomon built many cities. Kings and queens came to see him. One day the queen of faraway Sheba arrived.

She brought gifts of gold, spices, precious stones, and monkeys.

The queen asked Solomon to solve riddles and found that he was the wisest man she'd ever met.

Goodbye Israel. You have a happy kingdom and a blessed God.

But the happiness didn't last long. Solomon built palaces for his 700 wives and temples for their foreign gods. Taxes grew heavier and the Israelites started to complain. God said:

SOLOMON HAS FORGOTTEN MY LAWS! I WILL TEAR THIS KINGDOM AWAY FROM HIS FAMILY!

Solomon died and his son Rehoboam became king. A soldier called Jeroboam led a committee to the new king and asked an important question.

Will you lower our taxes and make our lives easier?

Are you kidding? I'll make your taxes even heavier!

It was the wrong answer.

Okay guys, follow me. We're leaving. We'll set up a better kingdom with me as king.

HURRAY!

Long live Jereboam!

Ten tribes revolted and left Solomon's kingdom. Only the tribes of Judah and Benjamin stayed with Rehoboam. Now there were two Israelite kingdoms-Judah and Israel. Many kings ruled over them. Some remembered the Covenant with God. Most did not.
Ahab, king of Israel, was one who did not remember. He married a foreign princess, Jezebel of Sidon, built a temple for her god Baal, and brought in 450 priests to serve Baal.

God sent Elijah the prophet to face Ahab and the foreign priests.

Come to the top of Mount Carmel. You, and all the people of Israel.

Now let the people choose between God and Baal.

The 450 priests built an altar and placed a sacrifice on it. Elijah built an altar too. But nobody lit a fire. Only the true God would set fire to the sacrifice.

The priests called and sang and cut themselves with knives.

They shouted and jumped and prayed all day. But Baal did not set fire to his sacrifice.

In the evening Elijah poured water on the altar of God to make it even harder for the fire to start.

Fire roared down and devoured the sacrifice, the wood, and the stones.

The Israelites fell on their faces and cried, "The Lord alone is God! The Lord alone is God!" Then they killed the priests of Baal.

But God knew what had happened. God sent Elijah to confront Ahab.

Have you murdered and then inherited your victim's property?

Because you have done evil God will punish you. Just as the dogs licked Naboth's blood in the field, they will lick your blood and Jezebel's.

Years later, when Ahab and Jezebel were killed, the dogs licked their blood, just as Elijah had predicted.

After Elijah came Elisha, a miracle-working prophet. Also Hulda the prophetess and many other men and women who spoke for God.
On the thrones of Judah and Israel, kings came and went. But only a few like Hezekiah or Josiah listened to the teaching of the prophets.

Elijah left the earth in glorious style. He was drawn up to heaven in a whirlwind, in a fiery chariot pulled by fiery horses.

King Ahaz sacrificed his own children to the fiery god Baal.

Queen Athaliah killed off her family so that she would stay in power.

King Manasseh built temples and shrines to foreign gods. He killed so many of his own people that the streets ran with blood.

God grew angry and disgusted.

I WILL WIPE JERUSALEM CLEAN! I WILL ALLOW ISRAEL TO FALL BEFORE ITS ENEMIES!

After a long war the Kingdom of Israel was conquered by Assyria, and many of its people were taken into exile.

More than a century later Judah rebelled against Babylonian rule. The Babylonians conquered Jerusalem, burned down the Temple and the royal palace, and drove most of the people away to captivity in Babylonia.

BOOK OF PROPHETS

ISAIAH

A vision of God came to the Prophet Isaiah, son of Amoz.

GO AND TELL THIS PEOPLE THAT THE KING OF ASSYRIA WILL SWEEP OVER YOUR LAND AND BREAK YOU INTO PIECES!

Isaiah went out to tell the bad news. His son Shaar Yashuv went with him.

Listen, people of Israel. The Lord says we will all be destroyed!

That's not fair. I bring offerings to the Temple.

You tell 'em, Pop.

I fast on every fast day.

What more does God want?

On your fast days you do business. You take advantage of your workers. You fight with each other. God says you should share your bread with the hungry and take the poor into your homes.

Let's go find another prophet. This one wants too much.

Isaiah warned the king and the people of Judah again and again.

Your hands are full of blood. Wash yourselves. Help the oppressed.

Or else you'll be sorry.

But they paid no attention until the army of Assyria invaded the land.

Give up! Your allies and your God can't help you. We're stronger than they are.

The Assyrians captured and destroyed Judah's walled cities. Finally they reached the walls of Jerusalem.

King Hezekiah of Judah called to Isaiah the Prophet.

How can God let this city of Jerusalem be destroyed?

This time you're in luck. God promises to save the city for God's own sake and for the sake of God's servant David.

That night an angel struck the soldiers in the Assyrian camp.

The Assyrian king raced home with what was left of his army.

But Isaiah had more bad news for his people. "Because you behave unjustly, the Lord will punish you. One day you and your children and your treasures will be carried off to exile in Babylonia."

Everyone cried and promised to behave justly. Then Isaiah had words of comfort for them. "The time will come when men and women will learn to live peacefully. And the wolf will live with the lamb, and the leopard will lie down with the kid, and the calf and the young lion will graze together. And a little child will lead them. They will not hate or destroy in all My holy mountain."

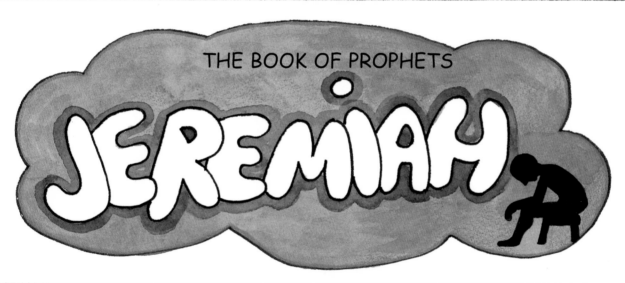

THE BOOK OF PROPHETS

JEREMIAH

The words of the Lord came to Jeremiah son of Hilkiah when he was still a boy.

I AM APPOINTING YOU TO BE MY PROPHET!

Me? No one will listen to me. I'm still a kid.

GO WHEREVER I SEND YOU, AND SPEAK. I WILL BE WITH YOU.

This I didn't need.

Jeremiah started his new career in the marketplace.

God doesn't want your sacrifices. God wants you to protect strangers, widows and orphans.

Mommy, look at Hilkiah's kid up on the fig box!

People laughed at the young prophet.

But as he got older they stopped laughing and started getting angry.

Liar!

Shut him up!

Stupid fool!

The destroyer is coming to ruin your cities. This is bitter punishment for your evil conduct.

Messengers began to bring frightening news to Jerusalem. The Babylonian army was invading the country. It was marching toward the city. The generals began to prepare for war. Jeremiah would not be quiet. They called him a traitor, a Babylonian spy.

Don't fight Babylonia! Obey God's laws. Respect Shabbat.

Suddenly a group of soldiers grabbed him. They dumped him into a dark pit and left him to die.

Jeremiah crouched in the cold mud and cried for himself and his people.

Jerusalem will become rubble, dens for jackals. The towns of Judah will be empty.

Just in time King Hezekiah sent servants to pull Jeremiah out of the pit. They brought him to the palace.

Jeremiah, I'm desperate. Please ask God to help us fight the Babylonians. God will listen to you.

"God will not help you," said Jeremiah. "The Babylonians will burn this city to the ground and you will be taken to a foreign land."

The Babylonian army besieged Jerusalem. For 18 months the city held out.

Finally the Babylonians broke through the walls. They burned down the Temple and took the people away to exile in Babylonia.

Then, at the saddest time, Jeremiah gave the people of Judah hope.
"Build houses and plant gardens. Marry and have children. And work for the good of the city where you live. If it prospers, you will prosper. The God who scattered Israel will gather the people in again. They will sing on the hilltops with new grain and oil, with sheep and cattle, like in a watered garden."

THE BOOK OF PROPHETS

In the Book of Prophets many prophets speak, warning Israel to follow God's laws, predicting disaster if they don't, and promising that God won't forget them, even if they sometimes do the wrong things.

EZEKIEL was with the exiles in Babylonia and comforted them.

HOSEA predicted the fall of the kingdom of Israel.

JOEL warned that a day of judgment was coming.

AMOS was a shepherd who defended the poor.

OBADIAH promised revenge to the exiles of Judah.

JONAH was an unwilling prophet (see his story below).

MICAH called on the people to do justice and love goodness.

NAHUM promised that God would destroy Nineveh, Israel's enemy.

HABAKKUK rejoiced in God even when Israel was poor and oppressed.

ZEFANIAH warned that sinners would suffer but God would bring the humble home.

HAGGAI declared that it was time to rebuild God's house in Jerusalem.

ZECHARIAH promised that Judah's enemies would come to Jerusalem and bow before God.

MALACHI reported God's words, "Turn back to Me and I will turn back to you."

JONAH

The lot fell on Jonah He confessed.

God is mad at me. Throw me overboard to save yourselves.

A great fish swallowed Jonah.

Inside the fishes' belly Jonah prayed.

Thanks for saving my life, God. I give up. I'll do what You want. I'll go to Nineveh.

The fish spat Jonah out onto the shore and he went off to Nineveh to deliver God's message.

Listen everyone. You have 40 days to do right. If not, Nineveh will be overthrown!

40 DAYS

Everyone listened! The king of Nineveh proclaimed a great fast and everyone prayed and promised to behave better. God decided not to punish them, which made Jonah very angry.

I knew this would happen. That's why I didn't want to come. Who wants to save stupid Nineveh!

40

Jonah went out of the city to take a nap. A plant grew up and shaded him. The next morning a worm killed the plant. Jonah was sad and grew faint in the hot sun.

God asked, "ARE YOU SAD THAT A WORM KILLED THE PLANT?"
"Oh yes," said Jonah.
"YOU CARE ABOUT A PLANT THAT GREW AND DIED IN ONE DAY," said God. "SHOULDN'T I CARE ABOUT NINEVEH, A GREAT CITY WITH THOUSANDS OF PEOPLE AND ANIMALS?

THE BOOK OF WRITINGS
PSALMS

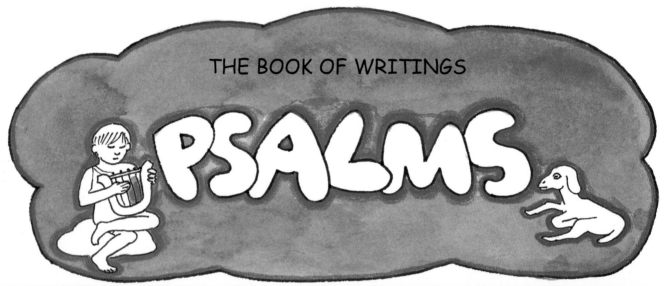

God is my shepherd,
I need nothing more.
God helps me lie down in green pastures,
And leads me by peaceful waters.
God revives my soul
And guides me along good paths.

Though I walk through a valley
Of deepest darkness
I am not afraid,
Because You are with me.
Your rod and Your staff
Will comfort me.

Let all the earth raise a shout to the Lord.
Burst into happy songs of praise.
Sing praise to God with the lyre,
With singing, with trumpets, and shofar blasts.
Shout before God, the King.

Let the sea thunder,
The world and all who live in it.
Let the rivers clap their hands,
The mountains sing before God.
Because God comes to rule the world.
God will rule the world justly
And its people fairly.

By the rivers of Babylon
We sat and wept
As we remembered Zion.
We hung our lyres on the trees
Because our captors asked us to sing.
"Sing to us songs of Zion."
How can we sing the Lord's song
On alien soil?

Hallelujah!
Praise God with blasts of the shofar.
Praise God with harp and lyre,
With timbrel and dance, with lute and pipe.
Praise God with loud, crashing cymbals.
Let all that breathe praise the Lord.
Hallelujah!

THE BOOK OF WRITINGS

PROVERBS

The proverbs of Solomon, son of David, King of Israel

The fear of God is the beginning of knowledge.

Better a meal of vegetables where there is love, than a fattened ox where there is hate.

Lazybones, go to the ant.
Study its ways and learn...
It prepares its food in the summer
and stores it at harvest time.

Like a gold ring
in the nose of a pig
is a handsome person
who has no sense.

A passerby who gets into someone else's quarrel
is like a person who grabs a dog by the ears.

What a rare find is a capable woman...
her mouth is full of wisdom,
her tongue with kindly teaching.
She oversees the activities of her household
and never eats the bread of idleness.

THE BOOK OF WRITINGS
JOB

Job was a good,
God-fearing man.
He had many sons and
daughters, flocks of
sheep, camels, oxen,
and a large household.
God spoke about Job
to Satan, an angel
who loved to argue.

JOB IS A FINE, GOD-FEARING MAN.

Of course. Why not? You blessed him with all good things.

Take everything away and you'll see how fast Job will start cursing you.

So God tested Job. God sent thieves who stole Job's livestock. Then God sent a great storm that killed all of Job's children.

But Job didn't curse.

The Lord has given and the Lord has taken away. Blessed be the name of the Lord.

Proudly, God said to Satan:

YOU SEE? JOB IS STILL VIRTUOUS.

Ha! Make him sick. Then he'll curse you.

"GO AHEAD AND TRY," said God. So Satan made Job very sick.

Oh God, why are these bad things happening to me? I've followed in Your ways. I've kept Your laws. But You have made my life bitter.

Three friends came to comfort and advise Job. But they were no help.

Tch, tch tch...

Oh, I wish I were dead! God, I cry out to You but You don't answer.

What a crybaby!

The Lord grew annoyed with Job's questions. Speaking out of a storm the Lord said:

WHERE WERE YOU WHEN I LAID THE EARTH'S FOUNDATIONS? HAVE YOU EVER COMMANDED THE DAY TO BREAK?

Right on!

HAVE THE GATES OF DEATH BEEN REVEALED TO YOU? IF YOU KNOW OF THESE, TELL ME!

Yessss!

How could I know of such wonders! But still, when I cry out to You, why don't You answer?

WILL YOU QUESTION MY JUSTICE? WILL YOU CONDEMN ME SO THAT YOU MAY BE RIGHT?

I'm sorry. I spoke without understanding things that are beyond me. I take back what I said since I am only dust and ashes.

Curses!

Then the Lord restored Job's fortune. Job raised a new family. And God blessed the later years of Job's life more than the earlier years.

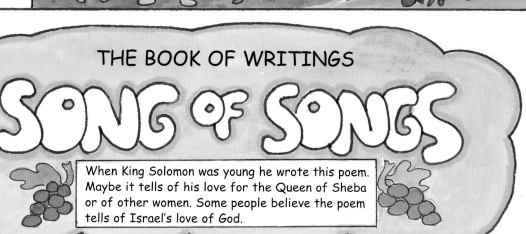

THE BOOK OF WRITINGS

SONG OF SONGS

When King Solomon was young he wrote this poem. Maybe it tells of his love for the Queen of Sheba or of other women. Some people believe the poem tells of Israel's love of God.

Daughters of Jerusalem, don't stare at me because of my dark skin. I am dark and lovely, like the tents of the desert, like the pavilions of Solomon.

I hear the voice of my beloved
skipping over the mountains,
jumping over the hills.
My lover is like a gazelle
or like a young stag.

Now he is peeking through the
lattice and calling, "Get up,
my friend, my lovely one.
Come away!"

Oh give me the kisses
of your mouth.
Your kisses are
better than wine.

The winter is past.
The rains are over and gone.
Blossoms have appeared in the land.
The green figs form on the tree,
And the blossoming vines smell sweet.
Get up my friend, my lovely one.
Come away!

THE BOOK OF WRITINGS

RUTH

Once there was a famine in the land of Judah. Naomi, her husband, and their two sons left Bethlehem in Judah and went to live in Moab.

Naomi's husband died soon after. Her sons married Moabite women named Ruth and Orpah. Then the sons died.

Naomi started packing.

Why should I stay in Moab, far from my own people? I'm going home.

We'll go with you.

Thanks, girls. You're sweet and loyal. But you belong here.

Orpah left but Ruth held Naomi tightly.

Don't ask me to leave you. Wherever you go I will go. Your people will be my people. Your God will be my God.

All right. Come.

They reached Judah at the beginning of the barley harvest.

I'll gather barley behind the reapers so we'll have food to eat.

Good idea, daughter.

The next morning Ruth went to the field of Boaz to gather barley. Boaz was a rich relative of Naomi's husband. In those days a close male relative of a childless widow had to marry her.

Who's that?

Naomi's daughter-in-law Ruth. The one whose husband died.

Work with my girls, Ruth. They'll protect you and you'll get more grain.

The barley harvest ended. Next the wheat was harvested and the grains were separated on the threshing floor.

Ruth, go to the threshing floor. At night when everyone is asleep, you are to lie down by Boaz's feet.

Why?

Don't ask questions. Just trust me and do it.

Well, good! Then, if she'll have me, I'll marry her myself!

Ruth agreed. Naomi was delighted. And Boaz and Ruth were married.

Ruth and Boaz soon had a baby called Obed. Many years later Obed's grandson David became the king of Israel. So Ruth the Moabite is David's great-grandma.

BOOK OF WRITINGS

LAMENTATIONS

These are said to be the writings of the Prophet Jeremiah as he mourned over the destroyed city of Jerusalem.

How the city sits alone
that was once full of people.
She has become like a widow,
she that was great among nations,
a ruler of lands.
She has become a servant...
All her friends have become her enemies.

BOOK OF WRITINGS

ECCLESIASTES

Some of the words of Koheleth, son of David, king of Jerusalem.

One generation goes,
another comes.
But the earth remains forever.
All the streams flow into the sea
yet the sea is never full.
What has already happened
will happen again.
There is nothing new under the sun.

Only this
I have found good,
that one should eat
and drink
and enjoy one's work,
because this is a gift
of God.

The sum
of the matter
is to revere God
and observe God's
commandments.

BOOK OF WRITING

ESTHER

Ahasuerus, the king of many lands, held a banquet in his capital city of Shushan.

Bring me Vashti, the queen. I want everyone to see how beautiful she is.

Yessir, your majesty.

Vashti, the King said to come.

No! I'm busy. I won't parade around for the king and his drunken buddies!

SHUSHAN TIMES

Vashti said 'no', your majesty.

She said 'no'? But she can't say 'no'. I'm the boss around here.

Get rid of her!

Disgusting!

Disgraceful!

Vashti is a bad example for the women of Shushan, your majesty. Soon they'll all disobey their husbands.

I guess you're right.

I'll have to get rid of her.

But then I won't have a queen. I'll be all alone!

Cheer up! Think of the fun you'll have picking a new queen.

A Jew called Mordecai and his beautiful orphan cousin Esther lived in Shushan. Esther was called to the palace along with the other young women of Shushan. King Ahasuerus fell in love with Esther and made her his new queen.
But Mordecai told Esther not to tell the king that she was a Jew.

Mordecai worried about Esther, so he would sit at the palace gate waiting to hear news of her.

One day as he sat he heard the two gatekeepers of the palace plotting to kill the king.

Mordecai reported the plot to the king's police. The gate-keepers were arrested, the king was saved, and the story was written into the king's records. At that time Haman became the king's chief advisor. He ordered everyone around.

Bow down to me!

Mordecai refused.

Not me! I won't bow, because I'm a Jew!

If Jews won't bow down to me, we don't need them. I'll get the king to have them all killed.

Esther was happy. Her plan was working. She rushed into the kitchen and arranged for special foods for the party. Haman was pleased too. It was an honor to be invited to a private feast with the king and queen.

That night Ahasuerus couldn't sleep. He had his secretary read the royal records to him. When he heard that Mordecai had saved his life, he asked Haman, "How shall I honor a great man?" He must mean me, thought Haman. "Dress him in royal clothing and lead him around Shushan on the king's horse," he said.
"Good thinking," said the king. "Do exactly that to Mordecai who sits at the palace gate."

Ahasuerus and Haman came to Esther's feast and ate and ate and ate.

117

King Nebuchadnezzar had plans for them.

Teach these boys our language and writings. I want them to serve me.

The boys were such fast learners that they soon joined the king's wise men.

One night the king had a nightmare.

What a miserable dream. I wish I could remember it. Ouch! I have such a headache!

He called his wise men and dream experts.

Explain my dream!

What dream, your majesty?

Tell us your dream and we'll explain it.

Idiots! Explain my dream or I'll have you torn limb from limb! Ouch - my head!

Daniel cried out:

Stop! Wait. Don't kill the wise men. Give me a little time and I'll tell you the meaning.

Oh God, please help me figure this out.

God came to Daniel in a night vision and explained the dream. Daniel went to the king.

All right, explain!

Yes, your majesty. In the dream God is telling you what will happen in the future.

You saw a great, awesome statue. Its head was gold. Its breast and arms silver. Its belly was bronze and its legs iron. Its feet were of iron and clay.

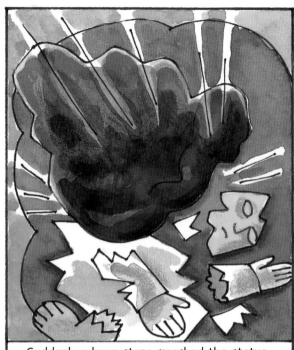

Suddenly a huge stone smashed the statue. The stone grew into a gigantic mountain that covered the whole earth.

Here's the explanation: You, mighty King, are the golden head of the statue. Weaker and weaker kingdoms will follow you. They will be smashed by a powerful kingdom that will rule vast areas and will last forever.

Your God who can tell the future must be the greatest God of all.

I want all of you to bow down to my statue. If not, I'll throw you into a fiery furnace!

One day the king had a golden statue made.

Gorgeous, right?

Beautiful.

Fantastic!

I love it!

Daniel's Israelite friends, Shadrach, Mishach, and Abednego, refused to bow.

Absolutely not!

God will save us.

Maybe God will save us. Maybe not. But I won't bow!

Nebuchadnezzer had them tossed into the flames.

Out they came the next morning without even a frizz in Shadrach's pony tail.

The king was amazed. Again he praised the God of the Israelites.

Daniel grew older, grew a beard, and kept explaining dreams. But he got into trouble with King Darius, who had conquered Nebuchadnezzer and now ruled the kingdom. King Darius decreed that his people could only beg favors of him-not of the gods.

Ha!

But someone overheard Daniel pray to God for forgiveness.

The man reported it to King Darius. Sadly Darius ordered that Daniel should be thrown into a den of hungry lions.

Before the lions could pounce, an angel of God flew down and slammed shut their eager, drooling jaws.

In the morning Daniel was freed. Darius praised the Hebrew God and told his people to tremble before God. All his life God granted Daniel visions of what was to come.

Yippee! I get the white meat!

Mmm... ketchup anyone?

Yummy!

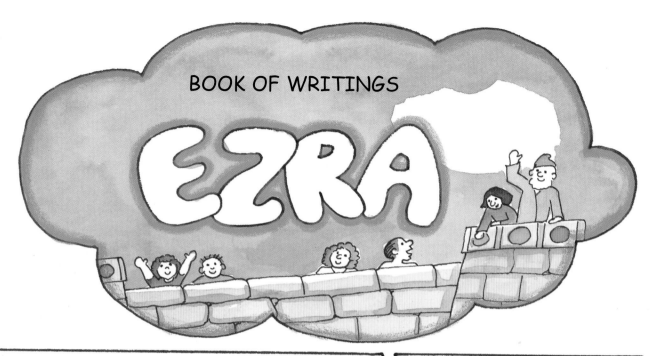

BOOK OF WRITINGS

EZRA

Many years after the Temple in Jerusalem was destroyed and the Israelites were taken into exile, a new king came to power. King Cyrus, the new king, proclaimed:

The Israelites may go back to Jerusalem and rebuild their Temple. I, Cyrus, will return to them the Temple treasures that were taken when Jerusalem was conquered.

Some of the exiles packed up and left. They crossed mountains, rivers, and deserts until they reached the land of Judah and the city of Jerusalem. Quickly they set to work to rebuild the ruined Temple.

The neighbors came to watch.

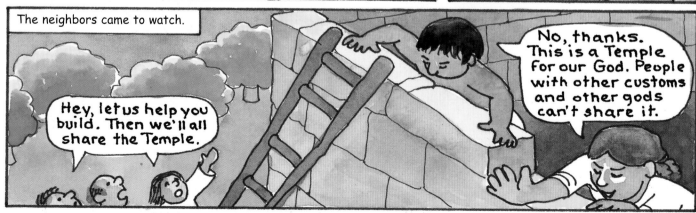

Hey, let us help you build. Then we'll all share the Temple.

No, thanks. This is a Temple for our God. People with other customs and other gods can't share it.

The neighbors complained angrily to the king. The Israelites had to stop building for a while. But finally the Temple was completed and they celebrated Passover together in their new house of God.

A learned scribe called Ezra rode into town. He was very unhappy with what he found in Jerusalem.

He was so unhappy and shocked that he tore the hair out of his beard.

You've taken foreign wives and husbands.

You're disobeying God's laws!

What have you done?

Ezra called a midwinter assembly. The Israelites stood in the pouring rain in front of the Temple and listened as Ezra scolded them.

You are forgetting the Torah! You must divorce your foreign partners.

We must become a God-fearing people again, living by God's laws.

And the people did as Ezra demanded.

123

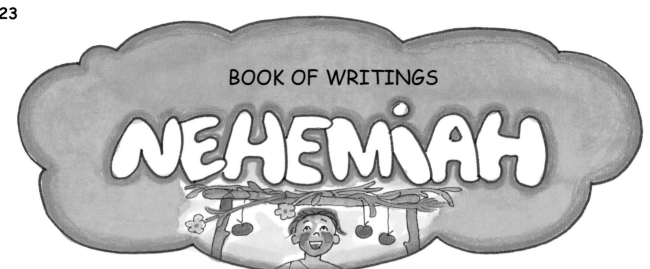

BOOK OF WRITINGS

NEHEMIAH

The king of Babylon had a Jewish cup-bearer. One day Nehemiah, the cup-bearer, was very sad.

Nehemiah, what's wrong?

Mighty King, I'm worried about Jerusalem and the Temple. I wish I could go and help my people for a while.

Go with my blessing, Nehemiah.

When Nehemiah reached Jerusalem he felt even worse. He wandered around the ruined city and cried.

Everything is in ruins. The Temple is defenseless.

Families of Israel, we must build a wall to protect the Temple.

Men, women, and children came, bringing stones, mortar, sand, and brick. They began to build.

The neighbors laughed.

Look at those bumbling Israelites. Their wall couldn't even keep out a fox.

The wall grew. The neighbors stopped laughing and began attacking. Stones and arrows flew at the builders.

Nehemiah set half the Israelites to guard the builders. The stone masons wore swords. The basket carriers held clubs. And the wall grew higher. Until, at last, it was finished.

On the seventh month all the people of Israel gathered in the central square. Ezra read the scroll of the Law to them and explained its words. "Amen," cried the people and swore to follow its commandments.

Now bring leafy branches and build booths, 'sukkot'. For seven days we'll read Torah and celebrate and share food with each other.

125

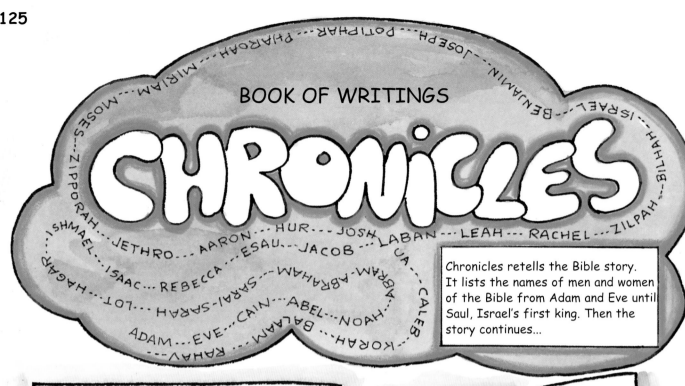

BOOK OF WRITINGS
CHRONICLES

Chronicles retells the Bible story. It lists the names of men and women of the Bible from Adam and Eve until Saul, Israel's first king. Then the story continues...

Saul and his son Jonathan were killed in battle against the Philistines.

David, the new king, captured Jerusalem and brought up the Ark of the Covenant.

David led his army against the Philistines, Moabites, Ammonites, and Israel's other enemies, and defeated them all.

He bought the threshing floor of Ornan on Mount Moriah as the site for the Temple. Then David instructed his son Solomon, the future king, to build God's Temple there.

King Hiram of Tyre sent lumber and skilled workers. King Solomon set masons and craftsmen to work. And the people brought gold and other precious materials. Slowly the Temple began to rise on its hilltop.

When the Temple was finished the Levites placed the Ark of the Covenant in the Holy of Holies. Solomon blessed the people and prayed for God's help.

Then fire blazed down and consumed the offerings on the altar. And the glory of God filled the Temple.

After King Solomon died the people came to his son Rehoboam and asked that he lower their taxes. Rehoboam refused. Ten tribes revolted and formed the kingdom of Israel. Rehoboam was left with the tribes of Judah, Benjamin, and the city of Jerusalem.

There were many kings of Judah and Israel. Some obeyed God's laws. Most did not.

King Hezekiah obeyed God and cleaned the false gods from the Temple. When the Assyrians besieged Jerusalem God sent an angel who destroyed their army.

King Josiah repaired the Temple and found a long-lost scroll of sacred writings. The Prophetess Huldah declared that it was Deuteronomy, the last of the Five Books of Moses. Josiah gathered the people, taught them the law from the scroll, and together they celebrated Passover.

King Zedekiah ignored the warnings of the Prophet Jeremiah. He rebelled against Babylonian rule. God brought the Babylonians to conquer Jerusalem, destroy the Temple, and take the Judeans to Babylonia as captives.

Seventy years later a new king ruled over Babylonia. He allowed the people of Judea to return home and rebuild their city and their Temple.

AN INDEX OF BIBLE PEOPLE

AN INDEX OF BIBLE PEOPLE (Continued)